£9.00

CW00408884

Of Sea-Graves & Sand-Shrines

A C BEVAN

2000

Published by Arc Publications
Nanholme Mill, Shaw Wood Road
Todmorden, Lancs. OL14 6DA

Design by Tony Ward
Printed at the Arc & Throstle Press
Nanholme Mill, Todmorden, Lancs.

ISBN 1 900072 46 7

Acknowledgements are due to the editors of the following publications,
in which a number of these poems first appeared:
Aabye; *Aabye's Baby*; *Holroyd's Poetry Monthly* and *Outposts*.

for Melissa

CONTENTS

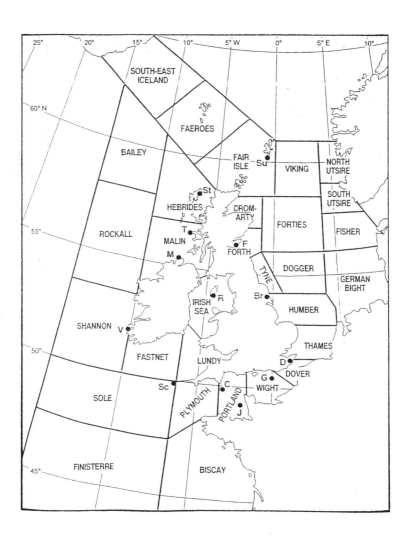

'The sea has many voices,
many gods and many voices.'

T S Eliot, *The Dry Salvages*

VIKING

Aphrodite's wingéd outriders
                are just a chapter of Hells Angels

called '*The Vikings*', who run amok along
                Bank Holiday sea-fronts

when by some process
of metempsychosis
you get transmigrated
or reincarnated
in the order
of coldwater
mudflat Crustacea,
viz.
as a species of
Decorator Crab,
which:
to quote the BBC
unit of
Natural History –
'...*bedecks itself*
with seaweed...
...to protect
its true identity...
...enough
to fool sea-bird
and octopus...'

but not gull us

and so
and thus,
finding yourself
on a cisatlantic
continental shelf

sea-kelp (!)

Famous Observations on Sea-Kelp:

'There is one marine production, which from its importance is worthy of a particular history.'
(Charles Darwin – *Voyage of the Beagle*)

'Lank coils of seaweed hair around me, my heart, my soul. Salt green death.'
(James Joyce – *Ulysses*)

'Enriched with natural extract of alga, to enhance condition and shine'
(Boots the Chemist – *Hair Products*)

FORTIES

and as I wept, I wept, I wept
you dove deep into the well
of inappropriate detail
to console me with the fact
that of the forty or more elements
that constitute sea-water
not one of them contains
– scientifically at least –
a trace particle of grief

CROMARTY

SS Moray Firth the Fourth
was built in 1954
and duly registered with the North
Sea Maritime and Shipping Board
and set her course
down the Firth of Forth
for oil-resort and fishing port
with her sister ship support network
of *Moray Firth the First* and *Third*

the *Second*
we reckoned
was jinxed and cursed
and lay at the bottom of Cromarty Firth
having ventured forth
in a gale force
and disappeared off the face of the earth
leaving an *SS Moray Firth*
the Second shaped hole in the Moray surf

FORTH

the first people to reach

      the / beached grampus

carved *HIBS F.C.* /

      in its dorsal fin

and stuck / a cigar-

      butt / in its gulping

blow /

      hole

TYNE

On my way back from the central, rental library with my plaid shirt on, in the park, alongside the river on the day Bukowski died, I saw a seagull drop a message into the pee-water soup, right there by the Beer Co. building. The bird message went something like this: 'Here is my shit. I can't use it any more. Do with it what you will.' And the river accepted the words with a stoical, unruffled *'plop'* (author's note – the reader understands that I was too far off to hear this literally, but onomatopoeically I saw the sound it made), and carried it downstream to, eventually, the ocean – the Atlantic more probably than the Pacific – where in time the atomic particles of the shit the seagull couldn't use dissipated into anti-matter and fossil-fuel, into the swim of the scheme of the evolutionary cycle of natural things, like all of us when all of us have died.
'No matter' said the seagull to the river.
'No matter' said the river to me, with my plaid shirt on.

NEPTUNE
A GOD OF THE SEA
ACCORDING TO ANCIENT MYTHOLOGY

THIS LEAD-COVERED STATUE
PRODUCED BY JOSEPH RENDALL
FOUNDER • BRISTOL • 1723
AND ERECTED ON THE SITE OF
THE OLD RESERVOIR OF TEMPLE
CONDUIT IN TEMPLE STREET
RE-ERECTED IN BEAR LANE
TEMPLE • 1787 – REMOVED TO
CHURCH LANE • TEMPLE • 1794 –
REMOVED TO THE JUNCTION OF
TEMPLE STREET AND VICTORIA
STREET 1872 •

ERECTED ON THIS SITE •
LATITUDE 51' 27' 06" NORTH
LONGITUDE 2' 55' 47" WEST
10TH MAY 1949 •

(and our dog likes to piss on it...)

FISHER

(or,
as I asked the sandwich-vendor
[who moonlights as the janitor
                                    at the Planetarium]:
is it true that all the tins
of tuna-fish ever consumed
would circumnavigate the moon
in an orbital of dolphin-friendly
                                    aluminium,
and thereby
solve the mystery
of Saturn's skipjack rings?)

GERMAN BIGHT

in shallow bays and bights
by night,

the phosphorescent algae
switches on its landing-lights

its sub-aquarium flare-path
to guide the passing aircraft

and relay in-flight messages
to cabin-crew & passengers:

the air/sea-surface
temperature;

the *FT* Index;
your ETA;

and: '***HAPPY 25th
WEDDING

ANNIVERSARY
ART & BESSIE-MAE***'

HUMBER

you built me a bridge
            with nuts and bolts;
windage factors;
            and tension-faults;

pre-stressed sections;
            and impact points;
lateral-bracing;
            expansion-joints;

you built me a bridge
            with supporting frames
on the horizontal
            and vertical plane;

continuous-trusses;
            suspended-spans;
force-bearing wires;
            and cable-strands;

a thoroughfare for traffic
            on either side;
you built me a bridge
            fit for suicides –

but I built you
            a bridge of sighs

THAMES

and you loved me

between
two riverine
bridges, between
Hammersmith & Putney
'twixt clutch of rush and reed;
there, where boat-crews rowed in teams
in compass, each encompassing
the laws of some Euclidean
scheme – then housed the boats
and home for tea
across hospitalfields, yes
and you kissed me here
beneath the old
gasometers
before the empty
depository of my dreams,
where sailed my heart
on a heart-sailed barge
carrying
its cargo of small longing
downstream,
down estuary,
beyond the tidal barrier
and out unto the sea –

and you loved me

DOVER
(after Emperor Yūryaku)

with her bucket, her bucket
and her spade, her spade
our seaside girl on the esplanade

with her flip-flip-flops
and her candy floss

her sticky-out stomach
and her polka-dots

she'll dig us a tunnel
right under the channel
and on to Australia
and on to new worlds

WIGHT

The giant chalk horse
on the side of the hill
grew tired of lying around
landlocked,
upped and thought: fuck it,
and in capriole bounds
went galloping south for the coast,
the spume of the surf in its nostril
the sweat-lick on wither and mane,
as over the saltings it came

you all know the story
of how it dispersed
the instant it hit the water
of course,
into thousands
of miniature
snow white horses,
in a starburst of limestone
a spindrift of moor

bipolar pit-ponies
steeplechasing the shore

PORTLAND

'Swell can travel long distances with little loss of energy. Only the wave form moves forward; after it passes, the water particles end up about where they were before. Individual waves are primarily described by their period, which is the time in seconds for successive crests to pass a fixed point such as a rock.'

(Willard Bascom: from *Adventures in Oceanography*)

'...For Your Enjoyment Tommy Matthews & Sons Proudly Present Britain's Traditional Galloping Horse Carousel...'

(Fairground Legend)

In the ground-swell
the sea-horse riders of disembarking waves
jockey for position, their white-caps buoyed
by underwater cables: under starters' orders then
'THEY'RE OFF!' at a rapid gallop
through the furlongs of the sea
towards the shingle finish line
– like the horse race stall at the end of the pier –
and in a photo-finish
the one you called the favourite
is first past the post, declared
the winner by a nose,
and trots back to the calm of the winners' enclosure
rosetted by starfish
and stewarded by gulls,
ready for the Portland Race.

On dry land
a small boy on the merry-go-round
is snapshotted forever.

PLYMOUTH

the lagan of my love lies off
the point
beneath a marking-buoy

beyond the cabletow
and the tugboat drogue
of the salvage company

sometimes –
my heart rides in on a flotsam tide
(my heart rides out on a jetsam tide)

to deposit something
of itself
midst the kelson,
bric-a-brac and shells,
pretty glistenings
which cost nothing

and so beachcombers come
collecting these small
        givens of the ocean
assuming it is merely coloured glass
        the sea has broken

BISCAY

already the days take on
a bygone of ultramarine,
a sense
of time passing
from historic present
to past tense, a series
of landing stages
of liminal phases
viewed from the observation deck
of an educational cruise –
where yet
still mornings came
on sea-planes, like
telegrams announcing births
in first
-day covers,
as erst
and former lovers
in a line,
(and trauma counsellors on the line)
for to plot a graph
with the sickle swathe
a liner carved
through the man-made bay.

FINISTERRE

dolphins
at the dolphinarium
saying 'cheese'
in dolphinese
and smiling for the cameramen

SOLE

so must I plough
the lonely furrow of my brow
cordoned in obscurity

as I lay me down to rest
in the surety and slough
of a life unlived. unliveable.

it was an easy death.
amongst the fields of the sea

the auroral light neglects
no Signal Immemorial
could repair me to the hands

that waved to me in streamers
from departing ocean steamers.

lone yachtsman that I am.

LUNDY
(*for Swee-Yong*)

because
your name translates
as: *Beautiful Clouds*,

they set the weather by you

the Meteorological Office
are issuing synopses
and posting them in weather-kiosks
throughout sea-bathing stations
because
you have the measure
in oktas of illimitable
sadness,
of beautiful clouds,

they set the weather by you

FASTNET

so
tore she from her sutures
and ran to find her sweetheart
in the tea-shops and the sweet-marts

and swam to find her consort
amidst the suitors
                    of the waves
in their undersea network
                    of grottoes and caves

only to be found
                    caught
fast
                    entangled
drowned

IRISH SEA

departing on the night-ferry
think not that it is we who leave,
but rather that some ferryboat
embarks upon its charted course,
to a tide-table of crossings
and re-crossings, whereas you and I
are fixed points in a harbour scheme
that twins the larboard lights
with the set constants of
                     the stars

SHANNON
(*i.m. Sarah E.*)

```
                                                              e
                                                              s
                                                              i
                                                              u
                                                              r
                                                             -c
                                                              e
                                                              z
                                                              o o
                                                              a b
                                                              n
                                                              l o
                                                             c a l
                                                              f
                                                              o
                                                              t s
                                                    o r
                                                  p
                                                r e
                                               w e
                                             t h
                                            w i
                                         t
                                      p
                                     e l
                                     s
                                   r
                                 e
                               v e
                             e   d
                          e    i
                        u'v    t
                 e          y o    r n i n g
                v r       e       o
        m e  o f e    y     n      m
      a     s         o      y
       n                    n k b
  if  e          e d r i
    th           h
                 t
          d o f
             a
      e' d b e d e

su   w
  re
```

ROCKALL

through strata
and sub-strata
of sedimentation

of alluvial
and diluvial
fossil-formation

geologists
can establish
with carbon-black-testing

paleolithic
mineral deposits
& pin point exactly

Where Things Declined
along fault-lines
& feldspars of glacial shift

in the prehistorical
obsidian world
presenting rock-samples, to wit:

&c.

MALIN

from medieval monks who'd light
their beacon fires on outlook cliffs
and pray for those at sea; through

keepers of the whale-oil lamp
with lens and wick and weather-eye
to train through scope and sextant, to

the unmanned offshore light station
with fog-signal and radio-mast
and electronic incandescent
equal-interval occultation
and short and long-range navigation
in land / sea / air communication

yet still our love is run upon the rocks

HEBRIDES

I don't know if long ago, ancient
archipelago civilizations
believed starfish to be
the manifest,
fire-extinguished husks
of celestial asteroids descended
from the azimuth,
and deposited on the shoreline
in some metamorphic locus...

but I sure-as-Jehovah do

BAILEY
(for Jo)

I lay in a glass-bottomed boat
in a bathyscaphe of instruments
and gauges,
plumbed
the gauzy fathoms
of an ultrasound lagoon

amidst the swaying sea-grasses
and coral-groves I saw,
at first
an aperture,
a fish-mammalian heart-valve
opening
and closing
occultating
like a pulsar from a sunken isle,
until
in subaquatic-time
a child-form stirred prehensile limbs
and swam quickly into liquid focus
surfacing to meet us
in a sonar-photograph

and that same heart
and those same arms
in a providence of sea pinks,
have brought you joy
untold
in depth
as divers fetch up treasure
from a wreck

FAIR ISLE
(for L. who could have saved my life but declined the offer)

it would appear I couldn't fathom you dear
I saw the sea-nymphs on the carousel
riding home, the moon mirrored itself
hanged from silver wires ear to ear

I saw you as a mermaid out of water
a seaboard siren singing to herself
begoverned by a moon I couldn't tell
the tide phased out and you the same as her

FAEROES

if there are moon-rocks beside an orrery
in the NASA Space Exploratory

museum at Cape Canaveral FLA.,
then surely by parallelism

there should be an exhibition
of golf-balls somewhere

in a moon museum
by the dustbowl Sea

of Tranquility,
in perfect co-
relati
vit
y

S E ICELAND
(Lines to the World-Weary Man I Saw on Channel 5 News Last Night, Who Has Gone to Live Alone on an Icecap)

I have fashioned a sled from an old pedalo,
and am teaming-up neighbourhood dogs.

with two tennis racquets for makeshift snow-shoes;
and '*Popular Mechanics – How To Build an Igloo*'.

I am loading a cargo of simple abundance,
small sorrows and cupboard-love,

to bring you the good news across the snow-fields:

this is all that we have
this is all that we have